From Grief to Grace

My Call to Prayer

Janet Wright

From Grief to Grace

Christian, Memoir

Printed in the United Kingdom

ISBN 978-1-3999-0117-8 (Hardcover)
ISBN 978-1-5272-9960-3 (Paperback)

Published by: Mothers with a Voice

Editorial Production: The Editor's Chair

In loving memory of

Corey Wright

30.01.1981 — 21.04.2001

Dedications

To my sons Andre and Gavin and my one and only daughter Chyna-Louise.

This has been a long, hard and painful journey for me, and we have been through hell and high water together as a family. Individually we have also faced many adverse and challenging situations.

I thank God for blessing me with the most amazing children and two beautiful grandchildren who mean the world to me. Thank you for supporting me through this; I don't know where I would be without you and I could not be prouder of each of you.

I pray that, as your mother, I have done enough to guide you on this road of life.

Don't ever forget where your help comes from, and that Christ is the head of our house.

Never give up on your dreams—aim high, the sky is the limit. Nothing is out of your reach and with God, all things are possible.

Always remember that I love you, but God loves you more.

Acknowledgements

First and foremost, I give thanks and all the praise to God, my Father in Heaven.

To Pastor Enid Stewart of Ruach City Church, I would like to say *thank you* for all your support and wise counsel during some of the most difficult and challenging times in my life. Never judging, but always with a word of encouragement. You would not know the impact you have had on my life, and I am forever grateful.

To Bishop and Co-Pastor Penny Francis of Ruach City Church, a huge *thank you* for the words you have spoken over my life. Thank you for your guidance through the word of God, your covering, teaching and undiluted preaching of the gospel.

Special thanks to

Dinah Knox-Hooke

Thank you for everything you have done and all the hours you have put in to help me bring my vision to life. Not once have you complained. You have humbly been by my side and gone far and beyond any expectations I may have had. I love and appreciate you. x

Elder Jessica Meade

Heartfelt thanks to you for your kind words of encouragement. Thank you for all your input and advice. God bless you.

Benjamin Howell

Thank you so much for giving your time and sharing your gift of photography. God bless you.

Billy McGhee, WAM Graphics

Thank you. God bless you.

Foreword

When Janet asked me to write the foreword to her book, I was taken aback but instantly agreed as I could not think of anything I would say 'no' to her for. She sent me the draft and I told her that I would start to read it. Little did I know that once I had started, I would not be able to put it down.

The pages drew me into a shocking world of rejection. They gripped me as I went through a myriad of feelings ranging from pain and anger at what she had suffered, to gratitude for those around her who had brought some respite to the nightmare ordeals of sexual and physical abuse.

Janet writes with such authenticity and transparency, which is what I love about the woman I once considered an arch enemy—yes, I am in her story and when my husband introduced me her on that destined day, she was by far a better person t' was. The love of God oozed out of her then as it still dc

Through the pages of this incredible book she mad instil a greediness, making you want to discover and v more about her tragedies and triumphs. You too will not be put the book down once you start reading it.

You have ever suffered abuse, made poor life decisions, been deep in mental health issues and need healing from traumatic life situations, then in this book, you will find answers and help as Janet takes you on her journey and 'tells all'. She allows you access to some deep, dark secrets and literally life-changing ordeals that few could have survived… but for God.

Jessica Meade

Contents

Introduction 13

CHAPTER 1 The Dreams 17

CHAPTER 2 Forced Ripe 28

CHAPTER 3 'We're in the Madhouse'. 40

CHAPTER 4 Why didn't I leave? 50

CHAPTER 5 The Reader and the Reverend 57

CHAPTER 6 The Darkest Day 66

CHAPTER 7 The House in My Dream 82

CHAPTER 8 'Give Janet a Plane' 94

Epilogue 103

Inspiring Verses About Grace 109

Notes 115

Prayer List 120

References 123

Introduction

I would go upstairs in my house when nobody was at home and 'tek to the bed', which I often did back then. There were days I was so weak that all I could do was cry and sleep. I was in total despair, grief-stricken, with no money and in debt up to my eyeballs. Nothing was going right for me. I was praying and believing God for so much but it was as if things just got worse. Yet I would dream, have visions, and God would minister to me.

He gave me many a word up in that room; I spent hours in there. On this particular day, I had a dream and as the dream came to an end, I heard clearly 'Read Habakkuk 2.'

I was not familiar with that scripture and did not know where to find it, but I reached for my Bible anyway and began to search. As I read the words, the Lord spoke to me. 'You will write a book and tell it all.'

'Write a book? Me! You're joking, right?' That was many years ago. I made many attempts to write this book over the years, but I just could not finish it. I cannot begin to tell you the warfare, the trials, the tests and temptations that I have been through. Well, finally, I *am* going to tell you!

But first, I need to let you know what God was saying to me when He told me to read Habakkuk 2. It was not until I took the time to study the book of Habakkuk that I finally received the complete revelation of what God had been saying to me all those years ago.

Habakkuk is one of the minor prophets and the author of this three-chapter book in the Bible.

In the first chapter, he asked God the question, 'How long am I to cry out with no apparent answers?'

In chapter 2 verses 2-3, God answered Habakkuk.

Then the LORD answered me and said, "Write the vision and engrave it plainly on [clay] tablets so that the one who reads it will run. For the vision is yet for the appointed [future] time. It hurries toward the goal [of fulfilment]; it will not fail. Even though it delays, wait [patiently] for it, because it will certainly come; it will not delay."

At that time, I asked God lots of questions. I did not understand what was going on in my life and I needed answers. God told me to have faith through these difficult times and write down the dreams and visions. He was telling me to wait; it will come to pass.

I eventually got to a place like Habakkuk. It did not happen overnight and it took a lot to bring me to this place where I accepted God's way and His word. You see, God controls the affairs of man, bringing good out of evil circumstances (the bad things that happen to us) and through our enemies.

God taught me that He is sovereign and will take and use those who sin against His standards and His word to produce His own perfect pre-planned will. Without being the author of their sin, in this case, even my sin.

Things may not have worked out the way I would have chosen but I can honestly declare (like Habakkuk) that I will rejoice in the Lord God of my salvation.

Accepting God's will, I am now confident in God, Who is my strength and enables me to walk in higher levels of trust and obedience. God has changed me; I am a different person. I had to get to this place before I could see how God was healing me, delivering and restoring me.

I thought long and hard about where I would start, what I would share and what I would hold back... Surely I could not tell my whole story. What are people going to think? What will they say? God knows they talk about me enough as it is already; this would really give them something to chat about. These are the things that often crossed my mind.

But each time I had those thoughts, I would hear the Holy Spirit so clearly say 'Tell all.' I would answer with a question.

'What do You mean?'

'Tell all,' I heard repeatedly. When I eventually started writing, and I was almost finished—so I thought, the Holy Spirit would say to me... wait a minute:

'Why fe you ears so hard?' (You know God has a Jamaican accent, right?)

'I told you to TELL ALL!'

'Ok, ok, Lord.'

I had to go back and add the bits I left out, so here we go!

They overcame by the blood of
the lamb and the word of their testimony.

– Revelation 12:11

Pseudonyms have been used in the place of some names.

CHAPTER ONE

The Dreams

I was born and partly raised in south London; the other part in Hackney, east London. I am the second youngest of seven children—my mum had six girls and one boy. My youngest sister, Veronica, and I were born here in the UK; the rest of my siblings were born in Jamaica.

We shared a house in Balham with my mum's best friend, Miss G, where we lived together as one family. I do not remember much about that house, but I know they later moved to Tooting and we moved to Camberwell Green. My early years were relatively normal; we still spent a lot of our time with Miss G and her children. We would all pile in the van to go to the seaside and many different places at weekends and holidays. I have great, fun memories of those times when we did not have much, but we had one another.

My mum had a soft heart for children—not just her own, but all who were around her. She would tell us about when she'd been in Jamaica and stories about Bredda Anancy, a character in many Jamaican tales. We would gather around, eyes fixed on her, taking in every word.

My father was a strict man, tall, dark and handsome. He always looked good and was well-dressed. You could smell his aftershave as he entered the room. He was a serious man; I do not remember him laughing much at all. My memories are of hearing the door open as he came home from work. We would run and sit down quietly; you would never believe that we had been running up and down the house playing and getting up to mischief just before he'd come in.

My mum would have his dinner ready, always hot, no matter what time he got home. There were no microwaves back in the day, so she would boil a pot of water, put the plate on top, and leave it there on a low fire. We would stay quiet until he went out again, which he did most nights.

I can remember sometimes waking up to him shouting about one thing or another, then I would hear stumbling and my mum crying. He hit her, and he did that regularly, for no reason that was apparent to me. I could not figure out what was happening. I was scared of him; we were all scared. When he fell asleep, my mum would wake us up, and we would run away to Miss G. We would stay a while, but he would always come and take us back home. I could not understand why we had to keep going back. The truth is that Mum was scared as well but had nowhere to go.

But one day, I think enough was enough. We left and went to Miss G. This time, when my dad came to get us, Miss G answered the door and told him to go away.

Miss G was not afraid of my dad and stood up to him. I remember them arguing, shouting... 'She is not coming with you tonight. Move from my door!' She stood in front of him, with my mum behind her, and she shouted, 'No more! You better leave before I call the police.' He left, cussing, but that was that and this time we never went back!

We moved from one place to another and were never really settled. There was a time that I was taken to stay in Birmingham with my grandfather and his wife. She was a nice lady but not very clean. I remember my mum coming to visit but ending up taking me home. She was so upset that I was not being cared for properly. I had sores in my head and I was chafed from not being washed regularly.

From about the age of five or six, I would spend most weekends away from home, with a lady I will call Miss K. She had a lovely house and two daughters. There was one other girl who did not live at home. I always looked forward to the weekends when we would play outside in the garden. We had lots of fun.

I had a close bond with the younger girl and some of my best memories are of the times I spent with her and the relationship we had. Later, I will tell you how it all became apparent and why we had such a special bond. Miss K took care of me; she treated me like her own. Sunday was always a special day. We would have a huge breakfast all seated around the table. There was always lots of lovely food—plantain, ackee and saltfish, fried dumplings, hard dough bread and everything you could think of.

For me, this was a real treat. At home, it would only be at Christmas and Easter that we'd eat a breakfast like that. We would get dressed up in our best clothes and the van would come and pick us up to go to church. I went to church every Sunday without fail; it was important to my mum that I went and that I was away from what was going on at home.

Someone told my mum that an old friend from Jamaica had a house with rooms to rent. We went to look at the house. I am not sure what the agreement was, but we moved into that house on Louisville Road. My mum cleaned, tidied and rearranged the place to make it nice. She put her stamp on that house and it became our home.

I think back to having to sit in the kitchen while she was cooking. I would have to pick the black bits out of the rice and shell the peas. She would tell me what she was doing, and I would have to watch and learn.

My mum loved to sew and had a little sewing machine she'd bought from a second-hand shop. Mum made the most of our clothes and almost all of hers. I would sit by her on the floor and as she cut the fabric, I would take the scraps and make clothes for my dolly.

She taught me to pray every night before I went to bed and to thank God every morning for waking me up. *As I lay me down to sleep, I pray the Lord my soul to keep; if I should die before I wake,*

I pray the Lord my soul to take. She would either sing or recite her favourite scripture, *The Lord is my Shepherd.* From when I was a young age, she taught me all those things; she was training me.

It was the summer holidays, and we would play out on the road. The common was down the other end of the street, so we could go and play there too. That was something we had not been allowed to do when we'd lived with my dad.

When we'd been with my dad, we could not go outside and play, even though the swing park was literally at the end of the garden. My mum would have to sneak us out. She would keep a watch while we played and if he came home and found us outside, there would be trouble. So, to be able to play and mix with other children outside was great. I would still go and spend time with Miss K; I would go to church and come home on a Sunday evening.

I was living on Louisville Road, where I have my first memories of dreams or more like nightmares. It was almost every night. I would hear my mum calling me, and I would answer 'Yes, Mum', but she never answered me back. I would ask her in the morning, 'Mum, did you call me last night?'

She would reply, 'No, I never called you, Janet.' I would even get up some nights and go into her room...

'Yes, Mum?'

'Go to your bed!' she would shout.

I had dreams where I would be falling down the stairs but never hit the bottom. I would wake up sweating with my heart beating loudly, terrified and crying. It seemed so real and I felt every motion of falling down the stairs.

Looking back, I think I had nightmares because most nights I went to bed terrified. You see, I not only shared the bedroom with my sisters but with mice. It seemed like thousands of them lived in there with us. I would go to bed crying with my ears stuffed with toilet paper to block out the sound of their scratching. Bedtime was very traumatic. Anyone who knows me well will know I have a terrible fear of mice, still now. I was a daydreamer, always thinking of myself as a woman with beautiful clothes and shoes, with a husband and children living in a big house with no mice!

My reality was that most of my clothes were hand-me-downs or the stuff our neighbours had thrown out. When it was dark outside, Mum would bring in the box that they'd thrown out and take out anything that she thought would be useful for me. One of the girls who lived next door was about the same age and size as me, so I would get all her shoes and clothes. The girls next door would often tease me about wearing the old clothes that they had thrown out.

At first, it had bothered me, but I got used to it and would tell myself that I would have beautiful new clothes and shoes of my own one day.

One Friday after school, I went to Miss K for the weekend as I always did. When I got home, my mum was not there, but I could smell smoke in the house. I made my way up the stairs. The smell was getting stronger and there were bits of ashes on the floor. I got to the landing where the kitchen was and noticed more ashes. I called one of the girls; their bedroom was next to the kitchen. 'Where is my mum?' The girl was standing there crying. 'Where is my mum?' I asked again and, 'Where is Veronica?' She said that there had been a fire and they were all at the hospital.

My younger sister Veronica had been burned very badly; her nightdress had caught alight.

By now Mum had remarried and as she later retold the event, Veronica had overheard arguing between her and my stepfather. So, to distract them and get their attention, she'd set herself alight to stop their argument. She had been taken to Queen Elizabeth hospital in Roehampton.

I remember us going to the hospital. She was in a special room and we'd had to put aprons and masks on to enter. There was the noise of a huge fan blowing and she'd been suspended from a frame above the bed. I still have that picture in my mind.

The doctor said to my mum, 'Mrs. Wright, I'm sorry, but I have bad news. We have done all we can, but your daughter is not going to make it.' She looked at him, wiping the tears from her eyes, and said, 'By the grace of God she will survive.'

She held my hand, and we walked out of the room. I did not see Veronica much after that. I was sent to stay between Miss K and Miss G's house for what seemed like forever.

My older sister Rhonda had left home by this time and was living in East London with her boyfriend. The marriage between my mum and stepdad had broken down and one day my mum just up and left! We went to stay with my sister in East London.

Veronica was getting better and was moved to the Royal London hospital which was not too far from where my Rhonda lived. She had a small one-bedroomed flat and we slept in the front room. It was not the best place to be but we had nowhere to go and my mum wanted to be close to the hospital.

Rhonda and I did not get on well and she would complain about everything I did. One night we got into a fight and she told us to get out of her house. It was about 10 pm, and we had nowhere to go. With our bags packed, we walked from Hoxton to the London hospital where Veronica was. When we got there, the visiting time was over, and the ward was in darkness. The nurse told my mum that we could not be there and we had to leave. Mum told them we had nowhere to go and told me to get into bed with Veronica. By now, all the nurses were saying, 'Mrs Wright, you cannot stay here!' and told me to get off the bed. I would get up, and my mum would tell me to get back in. It was late, and I was dozing off in bed with Veronica.

I must have fallen asleep because the next thing I remember is being woken up by a nurse who took me to a room where my mum was. They had arranged a bed for us to stay for the night, across the road at the salvation army hostel.

When we got there, I saw men and women sleeping in this large room; the smell was awful. The beds were low and all in a row close together. I do not think I slept much that night. We huddled up together in the bed, not letting the dirty blankets touch us and used our coats to cover ourselves. In the morning, we went to the bathroom to wash; it was disgusting! My mum splashed some water over my face and used the end of my dress to dry it then we left. We went back to the hospital, and from there, we were sent to social services. We were there all day. I remember them telling my mum it was time for us to go, as they were getting ready to close.

This time they called the police to remove us but as the police were about to take us, this one social worker came and said that they had found a hostel we could go to and stay in for the night.

The hostel was in Swiss Cottage. My mum had no idea how to get there but we took a bus, then another bus, and then we walked for what felt like miles until we finally got there. Every day we went back and forth from the hospital to social services and then we stayed in a different hostel every night until we were finally put in a bed and breakfast. After about a year or so of being in and out of different places, we finally got a house.

CHAPTER TWO

Forced Ripe

Our new house was in quite a nice part of Hackney. It was a conversion—we had the upstairs flat and an old couple lived downstairs. Everything was going well at last. My mum worked two or three jobs, early morning and in the evening. I was at a new school, and Veronica was making a slow but good recovery—though with eighty per cent of scarring to her body. It may have been as a result of the trauma she suffered, but my sister was also left with epilepsy and the learning difficulties she'd had before became more severe.

Still, life was establishing some normality. I would go to work in the mornings with my mum, and on the weekends we stayed with Aunty B. Mum had become close to Aunty B; they worked together during the week and partied together on a Saturday night. I spent a lot of time at her house, whilst babysitting after school and on the weekends.

The house was always busy. She had four children—three sons and a daughter; another girl lived with her as a daughter. They were all older than me but I made friends with the kids who lived on the estate. By now, Rhonda and I were cool again; she was now the best big sister you could ever hope for. She lived close to where I went to school and I would go there with my friends for lunch, mostly to show off as she had a nice flat and I was proud of her.

She had all the latest clothes and was very stylish, which meant that I was stylish too as she let me wear whatever I wanted and

I was spending more and more time with her. She would dress me up, put makeup on me and take me out with her and her boyfriend. I was going to clubs and dances from a young age; they would take me with them wherever they went.

I can remember them taking me to a dance and the doorman saying, 'She too young, me nah let her in,' but they always did in the end. That was where my love for dance and all the old-time music came from because I was introduced to it at a young age; some would say I was forced ripe! I was then twelve, almost thirteen years old. I had lots of friends and earned pocket money from babysitting and working with Mum before school doing early morning office cleaning.

One weekend I was at Aunty B's; I always slept in the back bedroom. On this day everyone had gone out, and I was asleep. I was woken up by feeling someone close to me, and I heard whispering. I was not alarmed at first, as the younger son slept in that room too. But today he had someone else with him. I could not see as the room was dark but they were now very close and touching me. I could feel a face next to mine kissing on me. His hair was soft so I knew who it was even though I kept my eyes tightly shut and pretended to be asleep. I began to feel scared; this did not feel right. I kept still, hoping they would leave me alone. Egging each other on, they continued to touch me. I could hear them saying 'You go first, no you go.' I will never forget what they did to me that night.

That was the first time I was sexually abused but it was not the last. By the time I'd reached sixteen, it had happened five times. Each time it was by people I should have been safe with, people I knew and trusted. Back then, many girls were taken advantage of and sexually abused. It was not only in Hollywood that these things were happening. If there was a Me Too movement in our community, the list would be endless. Nuff man would be going to prison for historical crimes of rape and sexual abuse.

I knew I was not the only little girl that this had happened to, however, for many years I never told anyone. I kept it to myself and got on with life.

My mum had told me all about her life in Jamaica. She'd been raised by her mother with no father around and had been one of seven children. My grandmother had a twin sister who'd been killed, so she raised all her children too. It was said that a woman had killed my grandmother's twin and cursed the women in our family down to the last generation.

Mum had also been raped at the age of twelve. Her mother had sent her to stay at a convent with some people so she could go to school. She'd been held down by one and raped by the other (sounds familiar—almost the exact same thing had happened to me and at the very same age).

I became rebellious; my behaviour was not good at all. I went completely off the rails, and I was out of control. I started going out with boys. I was never interested in the young guys in my age group, but I was always attracted to those who were much older than I was. I felt they could look after me, I guess. I was looking for love in all the wrong places.

When I was thirteen, I was involved in a fight in Haggerston Park while I was on suspension from school. One of my friends was fighting a girl. I do not remember what the fight was about but the girl was getting the better of my friend so I jumped in to help and hit her with my shoe. I did not know that the shoe had busted her head when I'd hit her, and she needed stitches. Someone who lived in the flats overlooking the park saw what had happened and called the police. We all ran off but later that evening the police came to my house. I was arrested and charged with grievous bodily harm.

On my return to school after the suspension, I was permanently excluded because of the incident in the park. I was placed on a care order and put in a home waiting for a place in Middlesex Lodge, a secure unit where girls were sent for bad behaviour back then.

The home was not far from my house so I would run away from there and go back to my home, but the police and social workers would always come and take me back. I overheard one of the staff members at the home saying that they were going to move me to Middlesex Lodge that day, so I packed my bag and ran away again. This time I could not return home because they would find me. So, I left and was on the streets. The company I was keeping was questionable, and I was on a path of self-destruction. Moving from one squat to another with some very shifty characters, I could not stand the things that were happening, so I went back to South London and lived with my dad and his wife for a while.

That move did not work out for long, and he sent me to live with Miss G... you remember Miss G from the early years? Well, after some time of being with her, she was no longer having a bar of my up and down and not going to school. She would say to me, 'If you're staying here, you have to go back to school, and this street life has to stop.'

At the time I do not think I was ready for all that, and I began to think about going back home to my mum to sleep in my own bed in my own room. I was fed up; I just wanted to go home but how was that going to happen? I had been gone a long time, and I honestly did not know how I could just move back.

Anyway, it was the 12th of December 1977, my mum's birthday. I made up my mind and plucked up the courage. 'I'm going home today,' I told myself. I rang home and Veronica answered the phone. 'Put Mummy on the phone,' I said.

'No! Mummy does not want to talk to you.'

'Put her on the phone!' Again, she refused. 'Ok, tell her I have a present to bring for her birthday, and I am coming down.'

I made my way home from South. I arrived at the door and rang the doorbell. Veronica opened the door; I ran up the stairs... 'Where's Mummy?'

'In her room. You can't go up there,' she replied. Ignoring her, I went up to Mum's room, knocked on the door and went in.

Now you know, back in those days we could not just go into our parents' bedroom. It was out of bounds but I went in and sat down. 'What you want, Janet? What are you doing here?' Head down, I answered 'I've bought you a present. Happy birthday, Mum.'

She did not even look at me or the gift; she just continued with whatever she was doing as if I was not there. I sat there with her in the room, and every so often, she would ask, 'What do you want?'

'Nothing, Mum. I wanted to come to see you.' The time went quickly and before I knew it, it was dark outside. 'I'm going to my bed, Janet. You better go back where you came from,' she said as she began to get ready for bed. I already knew I was not going anywhere, so I sat there as she carried on. 'Janet, you need to go.' By now, she was getting into bed.

What do I do now? I thought. *It is either I go or get in the bed with her.* Well, guess what I did? I took off my clothes and climbed into the bed right behind her. After all, I wanted to be home.

'Janet!' she called after me about three times. 'Get out of my bed; you're not staying herc.'

But she did not move, so I moved closer and closer until I was right next to her. I put my arm around her waist; she kept telling me to let her go and leave but she did not stop me holding her and eventually, we fell asleep. Things changed and I can tell you, this was the beginning of the most beautiful relationship a mother and daughter could ever have.

I was home, wow! *Happy* is an understatement to what I was feeling. We started right back where we left off; we had always been so close. I went and got my things from Miss G, and that was it, home!

I must have been there for about two months. One morning before Mum went to work and I was in the bathroom, she popped her head around the door and said, 'Janet, from you come home, you ain't see no period, you better go and look about yourself.' Period! Omg! I had not even thought about it but she was right. I had not had a period and I could not even think when I'd had the last one. Surely I could not be pregnant, could I? Nah, no way! But yes, I was pregnant and did not know what to do or where to go. I remember going to my friend's house that Sunday, and when I got there, she was in bed with an encyclopaedia on her lap.

I asked her what she was looking at. 'Come see this,' she said. She was looking at a picture of a baby in the womb and all the different stages of pregnancy. She told me, pointing at one of the pictures, 'This is how big my baby is.'

'Baby!' I shouted. 'Are you pregnant?'

'Yes,' she replied.

'OMG! So, am I!' We hugged each other and cried and then our cries turned to laughter. I was so relieved because I could share that I was pregnant.

'What are we going to do?' I asked. She told me about a woman at the school divisional office she had seen and said that I should come with her to see the lady and that she would take care of everything. So, the next day she took me to see the lady who organised everything. I had to get my mum to sign some papers, and on the 24th of February 1978, my 15th birthday, I gave birth. Yes, I gave birth!

Because I was over twenty weeks pregnant, I had to be induced so that I could deliver the baby. That was how the terminations were done. My mum and I never spoke about it; it was never mentioned again. We just got on as usual.

It was many years later that we were watching a documentary about terminations. They were showing a woman who was well over twenty weeks pregnant and how the abortion was done.

My mum said to me, 'Why go so far in the pregnancy and then do that? May as well she have the baby.'

It was then that I said, 'That's what happened to me, Mum.'

She said, 'No, you didn't have no belly!'

'Yes,' I said.

She began to cry out, 'Dear God, I never knew; I would have never allowed something like that to happen to you.'

After I had gone through my termination, I developed the strongest desire to have a child. Even though I was only 15, I wanted nothing more in life than to have children. It was something I dreamt about—having a family of my own. I did not think about much else. I was surrounded by babies and desperately wanted one of my own.

I never gave much thought as to who would be the father of the baby that I longed for and prayed for... yes, I prayed for a baby!

So, when I got pregnant at seventeen, I was over the moon. My mother was also happy until she realised who the father was. You see, she'd never agreed with me seeing him and did not like him. She told me that this boy was no good for me in no uncertain terms and that I could do so much better. 'Why would you downgrade yourself, Janet?' she would ask.

The relationship with my baby's father (if you can call it that) was not conventional. I'd met Travis at one of the dances we would go to every week. He was one of the guys that I use to dance with. He was a good dancer and would move my body to follow his every move as we danced. We just had this chemistry and before you knew it, that dancing had turned into something else.

Shortly afterwards I'd found out that Travis had another girlfriend who lived with him in his parent's house. I would call him and his mother would answer the phone and tell me not to call him and that I must not take his calls either. She would say to me, 'When Travis comes to your house, do not let him in.'

There was a time that I called and got into an argument with the girlfriend on the phone. I heard she was at college; people had told me she was some posh girl who was studying to be a journalist. They said he had a type—fair skin, slim and that we looked alike. I did not think we looked alike and we certainly did not sound alike. Even though she was cussing me, she was always well-spoken. I knew she could not manage me, though. I was in my element. Believe me, I had a foul mouth on me back then, and I let her have it!

But truth be told, I was sad about this situation and what she said to me stuck with me for a long time. 'You're just a common "chicken girl", you're nothing!' she said. *Chicken* was the name of the dance I went to every weekend, so I was fuming. Common! Hmm! Wrenk!

'Wait till I see you; I'm going to show you what this common chicken girl will do to you!' I said back to her.

After that, I never saw her anywhere. I did not get to buss her ass like I had wanted to. Trust me, if I had seen her, I do not know what would have happened. It would be many years later before we did cross paths again but I will tell you about later—where we finally saw each other and what happened.

CHAPTER THREE

'We're in the Madhouse'

When I think back over my life, I realise that God had begun to call me a long time ago. I'd always prayed about everything, but I was not going to church. I was too busy on the roads and in the dance. I always had dreams and whilst I was pregnant with Corey, those dreams I'd had started to come to pass. That whole incident on the phone with the girl, I had dreamt weeks before it happened. Along with many others, God would show me all kind of things which causes me to know that He was with me every step of the way, even when I made bad choices.

On the 30th of January 1981, 'Praise the Lord!' I screamed out as the baby was born. I had given that final push, and there he was, my son all 7lb 8oz of him. I was so happy; it felt like I finally had something to live for—he gave my life new meaning. I was a mother and I was going to be the best mum in the world! My mum was overjoyed; we were all so happy.

Corey Anthony Lee Dayne Wright sounded like a good name to me. I did not have much to do with Travis, and I did not care. Whilst I was out one day waiting on the bus to go home, I heard someone call me. I looked back, and it was him. 'How's my son?'

'Your son?' Some cheek he had. 'Tell me his name, and I'll tell you how he is,' I said as I kissed my teeth and got on the bus.

As Corey got older, though, he started asking questions. I did try to get Travis to be more involved in his life but he would constantly let him down. He was always coming but never showed up, always making promises but did not keep one. To see my little boy so upset was heart-breaking for me.

Corey would sit with his hat and coat on, waiting for Travis to come until he would fall asleep. 'Come and get ready for bed, Baba,' I would say.

'No, Mummy, my daddy is coming for me.' He would stay on the sofa till I carried him to bed. I would get mad and go down to the 'front line' where I knew Travis would be hanging out and I'd cuss him off! It never made any difference though; I just looked like a madwoman. Fed up with his constantly letting Corey down, I began to ignore him and erased him from my life.

I was relatively happy. I had a lovely flat that I'd made our home and was proud of. My mum supported me and some good friends who became family. I was a young single parent but it was cool. We supported one another and did the best we could.

Life was good. I took care of my son and supported myself by writing bad cheques (book and card) or *deets* as the younger generation calls them, so I was not short of anything.

My sister Rhonda lived a little way down the road from me; she also had a baby who was just a couple of months younger than Corey. We were together a lot of the time between my house and hers. One day, it was a Friday afternoon and she was excited that her older daughter who had been abroad with her dad was coming home. She left my flat to pick up her son from school and to see her daughter.

I was at home when I got a call from Rhonda's friend who lived in the same block as she did. 'You need to come, Janet!' she said. I could tell she was crying.

'What is wrong? What's going on?'

'Rhonda is on the roof of the flats. The police and fire brigade are here. The kids are crying; please can you just come now?'

I called my mum but got no answer—she was still at work. So, I got myself together, put Corey in his pushchair and ran all the way there.

When I got there, Rhonda was still on the roof. The police tried to talk her down for what seemed like hours, and eventually, she did come down. She was put in the ambulance and taken to the German Hospital. I gathered the children and went there too; it was not far—just up the road. I was confused about what had happened. When she'd left my house she'd been okay. She'd been so excited to see her daughter so what had happened in that short space of time to make her want to kill herself?

They had her in a room with a doctor for ages. The kids were tired and hungry and I was baffled from trying to figure out what was going on. The doctor called me into the room and explained that he was going to keep her in the hospital. He said that she needed to stay there so that he could assess what was wrong with her, and that they were going to be sectioning her. He left the room to sort out a bed. She was quiet, not saying a word, just staring.

Rhonda, 'Do you know where we are?' She never answered; I continued speaking. 'This is the mad hospital in Dalston.' She still did not answer so I said it louder. 'Rhonda,We're in the madhouse! And they are going to keep you here. You do not need to be here; there is bare mad people in this place! Come to my house, and we will talk about it. You will be okay. Please come with me, you can't stay here.'

Finally, I got through to her and she agreed to come home with me. When the doctor came back, I told him that she was fine and would be coming to stay with me. That she would be okay. 'She's just a bit down but everything's going to be alright,' I said. He warned me that if I took her home, it would be at my own risk, and I would be responsible for her. I replied 'Yes, yes, that's fine.' I wanted to get out of there. I got the kids together, and we walked home, stopping at the chip shop to get something for us to eat.

We got to my house and I put the kids in the front room and Rhonda in my bedroom. I dished up the kids' food, put some on a plate, and brought it to her in the bedroom. I left her in there to sort the kids out but then I heard her calling me. When

I opened the bedroom door, she was doing a headstand on the bed; I could not see the plate of food. 'What are you doing? Where is the food?' I kissed my teeth.

'Listen, man, stop the foolishness and get down!' I told her as I left the room.

'Janet, Janet!' This time she was shouting. Hmm, this woman was getting on my nerves. I mumbled to myself as I went back to the bedroom and opened the door… 'Get down!' I shouted. This time she was naked, 'Get down!' I shouted again.

'I am thirsty,' she complained.

'You need to get down and put your clothes on,' I told her.

'I need some water.' So, I left the room to get her some water. I tried to ring my mum to let her know what was going on, but there was still no answer. Rhonda was still shouting from the bedroom, 'Janet! Bring the water.' By now the kids were getting scared, and I was getting mad. I fetched her a glass of water, opened the door and there she was on the floor stark naked, legs in the air screaming as if she was giving birth.

'Are you alright, what is going on?' I asked. She was screaming louder and louder as if she was in labour. I cannot lie to you; I was terrified! I have never seen anything like it. She looked like she was giving birth! *What the hell is happening here?* I thought. As I got close to her, she grabbed me! The water went flying...

'You red bitch!' she shouted at me. 'Don't you hear me calling you?' The next thing I knew she was hanging on to me. I do not know where the strength came from, but I fought her off and ran out of the room. I called for my nephew to help me hold the door while I tied it up with a dressing gown belt. Huddled in the front room together with the kids, I cried. What was happening to my sister?

Okay, pull yourself together, Janet, is what I told myself. I began to talk to myself again. *Right, call Mummy*... still no answer, so I called the hospital.

The doctor told me, 'It is your responsibility, I told you not to take her. I am happy to have her back but it's up to you to get here.'

'Well, how am I going to do that?' I was crying down the phone. In the end, I called an ambulance, and after I'd waited for what seemed like hours, they finally came. It took them ages to get her out of the flat, but she was gone. I shut the door. Phew! That was one of the longest and scariest nights of my life.

The following day, I got my mum on the phone and began telling her what had happened. 'German Hospital! Janet, ah nuh de madhouse dat!'

'Yes, Mum.'

'Wha! An you lef ar deh?'

'Yes, Mum. She was going mad!'

'I am going to get my chile,' she said. I tried to explain to her how bad things had been the previous night, but she was not having it. Her mind was made up.

So, off she went. She collected Rhonda from the hospital and took her home, just as I had done the night before. I do not think she lasted two hours in the house with her before Mum took her back to the hospital. The nightmare ordeal had begun. I watched my mother pray and cry; she went through hell with her.

I remember going to visit her one day. When we arrived there, we could not see her anywhere... 'Excuse me, I'm looking for my daughter,' Mum said, asking one of the staff members in the hospital.

'She's over there,' he said. She was under a table, naked! My mum tried to get her to come from under there and cover her up, but it took some time until she eventually came out.

My mum was a God-fearing woman. I had watched her go through so much, and now this. She tried everything you can think of; she was at the hospital every day, bathing my sister, always praying; and she was just getting worse.

On another visit, again, we could not find her. This time they directed us to a side room. As the door opened, a terrible smell hit us. The girl with us fainted as we entered the room. Rhonda's tongue was swollen so big it could not fit in her mouth; I had never seen anything like that in my life. They said that her temperature was too high and they had no diagnosis. They also said that she was deteriorating fast! The doctor said to my mum, 'Mrs. Wright, I'm sorry, but we have done all we can. We have never come across anything like this.' He said that if he believed in witchcraft, this would be it.

Once again, I heard Mum say, 'By the grace of God she will survive,' as she wiped the tears from her eyes.

Rhonda did survive although she has never been the same again. I have had many more upsetting incidents with her over the years. I recall going to her house and seeing my name written on the walls. On another occasion, it was on pieces of paper in the children's shoes and pockets that I found whilst collecting them from the police station. When she was in that state, my mum and I were the enemies, and the fight was always against us.

Anytime she would relapse, while her children were young, I would look after them. Rhonda has battled with mental health all her life. We never found out what happened that day she left to pick up her son and to see her daughter and then ended up on the roof. I believe the enemy stole and destroyed her life and is still trying to do damage through our bloodline now.

Even back then, I knew we were not fighting against flesh and blood and that this fight was spiritual.

For our struggle is not against flesh and blood [contending only with physical opponents], but against the rulers, against the powers, against the world forces of this [present] darkness, against the spiritual forces of wickedness in the heavenly (supernatural) places.

– Ephesians 6:12

CHAPTER FOUR

Why didn't I leave?

In 1985 I had my second son; the relationship I had with his father Terry was again questionable. If I am honest, I had already gotten to a place where I'd decided that it was over. He was in prison, and I was fed up with his cheating. I often received random phone calls from people telling me he had another woman who was pregnant with twins. He denied it but I knew it was the truth, and so was everything else I had been told. I was finished with him. One night I came home to find Terry in my room. He was in bed. My sister had let him in while I was out; one thing led to another and soon after, I found out I was pregnant. I was happy to be having a baby, as I was still caught up in this idea of building the family I have always wanted. Terry, on the other hand, was not happy at all. He treated me badly and would say that the baby was not his because of the rumours he'd heard about me seeing someone while he was away.

Why didn't I leave? I asked myself this many times; I had choices and opportunities to do so much. I was modelling on and off and if I had continued, who is to say how far I would have gone. But my desire to have a family far outweighed my desire to be a model; being a mother was more important to me. It was only a few months after having the baby, and guess what...? I was pregnant again! 'My God, Janet, you have not had one good night's sleep, and you're looking to have another baby!' Those were my mum's words to me when I told her that I was pregnant. When I told him, he was furious!

Daily he would come by and harass me. 'Hold on, you still got that belly,' he'd say as he poked me with his foot. He would be nice one minute and the next, he would switch. I could not stand it; yet, I loved him and had these dreams that we would one day be a happy family. I did not know how I was going to manage, but I had friends who had babies close in age, and they were managing well. If they could do it, so could I! All I needed was my mum's support and I would be fine, were my thoughts.

After being constantly bullied by him, I guess I'd had enough and booked to have an abortion. I was in the hospital, I'd signed all the papers, met the anaesthetist, and was ready to go but deep down I knew I did not want to go through with it. I went to the payphone and called my mum. 'What is it, Janet?'

'Nothing, Mum. I'll call you back.' I called her about three times, and each time said the same thing. I went back to the ward and was waiting for my turn to go down. All the while I was crying to God. I did not want to abort my baby, but I felt I had no choice. Then it was as if God answered my prayers. Coming around the corner was a friend and his girlfriend. They'd come to visit me. They were Terry's friends but we had become close and built a friendship. 'What are you crying for?' they asked.

'Nothing,' I answered but I just could not stop crying.

'Why are you crying?' they asked me again. This time I told them that I did not want to be there and that I wanted to have my baby. 'Well, get up! Put on your clothes, and let's get out of here.' I could not get up and dress quickly enough so that I could get out of there.

They took me home and my mum was there. She had been looking after the kids for me. All she said was, 'You must know, Janet Wright.' She always called me by my full name when she was making a point. I was relieved and happy to be home and I made up my mind I was having my baby.

Everything was going to be alright, but I still had to face him. He was angry, and he did not hide it. He would come round and I would be on the sofa lying down. He would lie down at the other end. I remember thinking, *Hmm, he is in a good mood*, but I was wrong. He would poke my belly. 'You still got that belly; you better get rid!' I was under so much pressure and stress; this man was horrible and made me feel awful.

On the 4th of June 1986, my third son was born. I woke up early that morning with a pain in my stomach. I did not feel well, so I thought I would go back to bed for a bit. However, the pain did not go away and was getting worse, I was only twenty five weeks pregnant so how could this be labour? It was too early, although I knew how I felt.

I stayed in bed for a while, but the pain was too much, so I called the hospital. They told me that I could not be in labour, but if I insisted, I should come to the hospital to get checked out. As I was getting ready to go, Terry came to the flat with his face vexed as usual. No 'How are you?' No 'What is the matter?' Just the same abuse. I told him that something was wrong and I heard the door slam. He had left.

There I was, crying from the pain but crying for him too. By the time I got to the hospital, I was almost fully dilated and the baby was coming. The hospital told me that they did not have the facilities to care for such a tiny baby so I had to be transferred to University College Hospital. They have a special baby care unit—one of the best in the county. With sirens and blue lights flashing and blaring, the ambulance took me to the hospital and at 7.15 pm that evening, the baby was born. He was breach and weighed a little over 1lb. Yes, that is what I said—1lb!

The doctor came to speak to me and gave me a polaroid photograph of the baby. He told me that he was small and could not breathe for himself as his lungs were not fully developed. They would do all they could, but the next few hours were critical and they did not expect him to survive.

I lay in that bed and cried and cried. I was broken and thinking about how badly this man had treated me, but still wanting him and waiting for him to walk in the door. He never did.

I prayed and asked God to give me strength because I was weak. I was so low that I did not know how I would get through this. I was finished! It was then I heard God say to me that the baby would be okay. It was as if God had to take him from my womb because he was not safe there. I was not strong enough to carry him full term and in the neonatal unit, they would take care of him.

Concerning this, I pleaded with the Lord three times that it might leave me; but He said to me, My grace is sufficient for you [My loving kindness and My mercy are more than enough always available regardless of the situation]; for My power is being perfected [and is completed and shows itself most effectively] in [your] weakness. Therefore, I will all the more gladly boast in my weaknesses so that the power of Christ [may completely enfold me and] may dwell in me. So, I am well pleased with weaknesses, with insults, with distresses, with persecutions, and with difficulties, for the sake of Christ; for when I am weak [in human strength], then I am strong [truly able, truly powerful, truly drawing from God's strength].

– 2 Corinthians 12:8-10

God was true to His word, and my baby survived. Blind in one eye and partially sighted in the other, he was diagnosed with cerebellar ataxia; he also had a perforated stomach that needed emergency surgery. I had signed the consent, and they took him to the theatre, but he was back in no time without having had the surgery. They could not find the perforation—it was gone! My God. The doctors said that he would never walk, never eat solid food, the list was endless concerning what they said was wrong with him. We went through years of going back and forth to the hospital with him.

At the age of five, he was run over by a car and almost killed. He had terrible injuries and had to learn to walk again, but he survived them all. Throughout his life, the hand of God was on him; God kept him, you would never know the daily challenges he faced. He has the strongest will, with the biggest, gentlest heart. He overcame every single obstacle that came his way, all by the grace of God.

CHAPTER FIVE

The Reader and the Reverend

I moved from my little flat on the estate to a lovely four-bedroomed house. I could not believe it—it had been completely refurbished, brand spanking new. Thank You, Lord! Again, I saw how God had blessed me with this house. I did what I could to make it nice and y mum helped me like she always did. The house was now completely decorated, furnished and looking good. The picture I had of my family was almost complete; all that was missing was the man. I still wanted Terry and was prepared to accept him back, no matter what had happened.

He eventually moved in with me, but it wasn't long before he returned to his womanising and abusive ways. On the outside, things looked great but behind closed doors, it was a disaster. It seemed like I constantly had a black eye or busted lip.

We would fight over everything; I would hit back too and cuss a string of bad words. I was not going to let him just beat me up without defending myself. But I soon realised that I couldn't fight him—he was bigger and stronger than me, and the more I fought, the more injuries I had. So, I stopped, but he never did. He beat me up regularly. He would go out on a Saturday night and come home on Sunday afternoon from the dance. I'd be cooking in the kitchen, the kids would be playing, and he would expect me to leave the cooking and the kids and come to bed in the middle of the afternoon. He didn't care—he would drag me upstairs if necessary, before forcing me to sleep with him. This happened regularly; the women, the beatings and forcing me to sleep with him. I felt like I was useless, a doormat and worthless.

We did have some good times, and I always hoped that things would get better, but they never stayed good for long. I remember one day he was in the front room playing music. Terry had some money from his mother, I think. She had sold her house. I had some savings, too; I was still writing the bad cheques, 'book and card'. This was how I took care of myself and the kids, kept the home together and paid all the bills.

I went into the room, and I said to him, 'I think we should get married. You've got some money, and I've got some, so we have enough for a wedding.'

'Married, marry who? You!' He laughed in my face. 'You must be mad! I soon get my flat!' This is what he said to me.

I was furious! I screamed, 'Get your flat, you need to get of my house, get out now!' I don't think I need to detail what happened next; let's just say I was sporting another black eye and busted mouth by the end of it.

Something changed in me; it was time to call it quits and get out of this relationship. This man was not going to change. He did not love me and meant me no good. Once again, I decided that I was done, but for real this time. The problem I faced was how was I going to get him out. Although he'd said he would soon get his flat, he didn't seem to be going anywhere fast. I would get on with things, cook and clean as usual but trust me, I had shut down. I hardly spoke to him; I just changed. He took my actions as rejection and became very angry. I was trying to work out how I was going to get him out of my house. I started going out more and spending time with friends. In my desperation and not knowing what to do, a friend told me that there was a woman I could go to who could tell me my future. She made me an appointment, and I went to see her. She was an old English lady, quite sweet. I sat down and she began to tell me all about my life. She also told me all about Terry, calling him by his name. I almost fell off the chair. To cut a long story short, she told me he would leave but not before he hurt me badly this time. Well, just as she told me, the time came, and for one reason or another, we got into it but this time I woke up in hospital with a broken nose. This was something he used to threaten me with. He would tell me whilst running his finger down my nose... 'I'm going to break that pretty little nose you got before I leave you.'

I had a broken jaw, fractured cheekbone, and a string of other injuries. But it was over; Terry left the house, and he was not coming back this time. It would be the last time he put his hands on me.

What I didn't know was that by going to get the reading, I had opened the door and given access to the devil to think he had authority over my life. I was desperately seeking answers and almost became addicted to finding out what was coming next for me. With my dreams of a family shattered and over, I was determined to get back on my feet and take care of myself and my children.

I was in a bad way physically, mentally and emotionally. A mess. My friend had told me about a Reverend she knew and said that I should come to see him with her. I remember going to his office; I was wearing sunglasses because I still had bruises from my injuries. My eye would not fully open. I had been seen at St Bartholomew's Hospital and was on the waiting list to have surgery to fix my fractured cheekbone. I went into the office and sat down with my sunglasses still on, as he began talking to me, telling me that God had a plan, and there was a call on my life. He said that I was not to have the surgery because God would heal me. Then he said that I would spend some time in prison, but I should pray and God would deliver me. By this time I was thinking that this man was crazy and I could not wait to get out of there.

Prison, me? That is impossible. By now I had stopped writing cheques and anything else I'd been doing that could get me into trouble with the police, but so said, so done. I hired a car for someone, and they did something wrong in the vehicle. Someone had taken the registration number and passed it over to the police, so it all came back to me.

The police came and arrested me, and I ended up in Holloway Prison. I could not believe it; the whole time I was there, all I could think about was what the Reverend had told me. So, I began to pray and read the Bible. While I was in prison, I had time to think about my life and my children. I decided that things had to change when I got out; I could not go through anything like this again. People heard what had happened to me. There was one person, in particular, a long-time friend I had known for many years. There had never been anything between us; we were just friends, but he would come to the prison to visit me almost every day. He sent me money and anything else I needed plus flowers daily along with magazines and a newspaper. Again, just like when I'd had my last son, God spoke to me and told me that He'd had to get me away from all that was going on at home so I could think straight and make sure there was no going back to that relationship.

The time I spent in prison changed my life for the better. I had all the time in the world to focus on myself. Being away from my children was not easy though and I missed them so much. However, I was getting to know God and learning to pray for myself.

I stood on the scriptures the Reverend had given to me. Two months later, I went to court for a routine hearing. This time, the officer in the case visited me in the cells and said they would not object to bail, so I should apply. I could not believe what I was hearing. My friend raised the bail money to give to my mum, and I was out! I could not wait for Sunday to go to the Reverend's church; everything he had said came to pass.

God began to change me, and I saw breakthrough and deliverance take place in my life. Prayer became a significant part of my life, and little by little, things started to fall into place.

The friendship between my friend who had been so good to me while I was in prison had now turned into something more and we started dating. I was having a great time 'living my best life', as they say. I was not used to being treated like this by a man. I had always taken care of myself, paid all the bills and taken care of everything myself. Now I had someone being so kind to my children and me, but it was hard for me to accept and caused some conflict. It was not long before I was head over heels and wanted more from the relationship. My hope of building a family and having more children was back. However, realistically, it would never happen with who I was with because he was attached to someone else and had no intentions of settling down with me. So as hard as it was, I ended it and took some time out to get myself together.

I started going on dates and met some great guys. I began dating a well-known boxer back then but I never thought he would take me seriously with it all being a 'secret'. *Is he honestly going to want me with three children?* I would ask myself. I felt like I was wasting time. My self-esteem was on the floor, and I had no confidence.

I took counsel from the Reverend when he suggested I come and start a program he was teaching called *Lessons in Truth*. I also attended college on a training course to become a counsellor. I thought about all that I had been through and wanted to do something positive with the things I'd experienced.

I was focused and putting the things I had learned into practice. One of my closest friends lived in temporary accommodation with her children, waiting to be rehoused. One morning as I was on my way to college, I noticed a billboard near the end of the road. The council was building new homes—two, three and four-bedroom houses. Morning and evening, as I walked by, I would pray 'God, I'm asking You, can You give my friend one of these houses? You said that if I ask anything in Your name, it shall be done. I declare in Jesus' name that one of these four-bedroom houses will belong to her.'

I kept praying and kept believing that God would give her the house. I had to convince her that God would give it to her, which was not an easy task considering she was a Rastafarian and had different beliefs.

I told her not to accept any offers of housing from the council because this was where she was going to live. 'It is yours in Jesus' name,' I would tell her over and over.

She would call me and say, 'Jan, they sent me an offer.'

'Refuse it!'

'But they said it's my last offer.'

'Refuse it!'

I think it was about a year and a half later that she called me again. I could hear the excitement in her voice. 'You're never going to believe it, guess what...'

'You've got the house down the road!'

YES, YES!' she exclaimed.

'I told you God was going to give it to you.' I can't begin to tell you how happy I felt. That took my faith to a whole other level and planted a seed in her that would grow and bear much fruit.

CHAPTER SIX

The Darkest Day

I met the man of my dreams; you know that song by CeCe Peniston, *Finally*? Well, I met my Mr Right! The lyrics sum up exactly how I felt. Wade was different from anyone else I had dated in the past; he had a presence that commanded respect without saying a word. He was well-dressed and always smelt great, *a true gentleman* is how I would describe him, and we became friends.

This is the man for me, God had sent him, I told myself. After all, I had been praying for the right man to come along, unbeknownst to him. I had made up my mind that I would look no further; this was it for me. I had it all worked out; the family life that I had longed for was finally going to happen. I had my boys, but the desire for a daughter had become stronger than ever. Wade seemed to be the perfect man to be the father of my daughter. Things were not bad, but looking back, I realise that I had grown complacent with a relationship that had promised me nothing. Sometimes I wouldn't see him for weeks, but at the time I was okay with that. Growing up, he had not had much love in his life, and as we talked about his past, it made me just want to love him and take care of him. That's what was missing and I was going to fix it. When really, it is what I needed, and I craved for somebody to love me.

I didn't think about myself; my focus was on him. Pleasing him was my priority; I was determined to be that 'everywoman' for him. I worshipped the ground that he walked on. Wade travelled a lot, so we did not spend much time together. I guess I was so blinded that I could not see what was going on. I was just happy to be with someone like him who seemed to be the perfect match for me. He was honest and never made any promises to me. He would say, 'Let's just try and see how it goes.' It was not long before I was pregnant and it was one of the happiest times of my life. Wade also seemed to be happy, which was a first for me; to have his support meant everything.

I was still going to church but had one foot in and the other out and was embarrassed to tell my pastor I was having a baby. The time came, and I went to see him. I sat in the chair with my head down; I was so ashamed, but he was kind and told me that children were a blessing from God, I would have this little girl and have no more children. He said, 'Janet, you did not ask God before you gave this man your heart,' and he was right. I prayed about everything but hadn't asked God before giving my heart away. I was convinced this man was the answer to my prayer and now being pregnant was what I wanted more than anything.

The pregnancy was not easy; I spent most of the time in the hospital on bed rest. I was unable to complete the counselling course even though I had got to the last part.

My beautiful baby girl was born on the 13th of July 1993. Thank You, God! With Wade by my side through the birth, I loved and respected him even more. My dreams of this beautiful family were well on the way despite the many red flags in my relationship. I would not give up, though. *It will be okay*, is what

I told myself. So, I began to focus on a bigger house, somewhere we could live together and raise the children.

For two years, I prayed and stood on the word of God and believed I was going to move. I would walk to the area I wanted to live in and pray. I started buying new things to get ready for my new home. To some, it was a joke. 'You've got a lovely four-bedroomed house. Do you believe you'll get another one? You're crazy!' But I knew whatever I asked God for according to His will, believing that I would receive it, would be mine. So, I didn't stop praying until I got that house.

Newly refurbished, bathroom and shower room, a beautiful garden—it was more than I'd asked for; more than I could have ever dreamed of. The house was on a lovely little road and I had the best next-door neighbour who became a great friend. God had come through for me like He always did and before long, Wade and I were living together. This was about as good as it was going to get.

I was home with the kids alone most of the time, as he would spend weeks away on 'business'.

Initially, this was fine but his being out more than at home got to me. My mum still spent most of her time with the kids and me but I felt lonely and unloved. I lived like a single parent; he was never there. *It will get better*, I told myself; *he is trying to make a better life for us.* So I didn't complain. I made sure that he was happy when he was home, and that was that.

Things, however, were about to take a downhill spiral and nothing could have prepared me for what was about to happen. It was springtime and Corey was sixteen years old. He was a typical teenager—quite popular amongst his peers, tall, handsome and funny. He had got into a bit of trouble here and there that I put down to adolescence, but overall, he was a good boy. We had a close relationship, and there wasn't much he didn't share with me. He had a close-knit group of friends that would come over to our house most days.

On this particular day, I remember him and his friend telling me they were going to the hospital; someone they knew had been stabbed. The events that occurred after would turn my life completely upside down. Corey, alongside several other boys, got arrested.

After he and his friend left the hospital, they went to the Carlton Lodge estate. He told me that as they'd pushed the door to the stairwell that led to the roof, they'd heard gunshots. The police made arrests based on the names the victim's friends had given them. Many of those names were not even there, but they all ended up in prison on remand. Corey was one of them.

I made the journey to Feltham every day and encouraged Corey, telling him that everything would be okay, that he was innocent and would be vindicated once the case went to trial.

I prayed, fasted, and supported him all the way, but it wasn't okay. The prosecution changed the charge. Corey was found guilty of conspiracy to commit grievous bodily harm and sentenced to six years in prison; the boys who pleaded guilty were given four years. One person pulled that trigger and ruined so many lives. I did not understand it then, and I still don't understand it now. I was angry at God—how could He have let this happen? It was the worst thing that could have happened, or so I thought.

Corey used his time in prison to further his education. He studied hard and achieved a lot. He came home from prison, a man with lots of dreams and aspirations to make something of his life. He started to pursue his goals and catch up on the things he had missed out on. I was happy he was home but deep down, I always feared something happening to him. I couldn't sleep until he got home. So, I moved him out of the area. He was reluctant to go but I thought it would be best and safer for him. There had been several killings over the years and one of Corey's good friends, Mena, had been killed.

Corey didn't seem worried or afraid of anything; he was focused and getting on with life. We talked about any and everything. One of the things he would say to me all the time was, 'Don't worry about me, Mum, I'm not going back to prison, and the police will never get their hands on me again unless I'm in a body bag! And I'm not ever having any children.' He joked that the only way that would happen was if he married Beyonce Knowles.

During that time, my relationship with Wade was on the verge of a breakdown. We had gone away to Spain for a break to see if we could rekindle our relationship; this was the last attempt to see if we could save it. Well, that did not work, and I made up my mind it was over.

That last day in Spain was so tense that not a word was spoken between us. We got home, I put the key in the door, and the phone was ringing. It was about 6 am, who could be calling at this hour?

'Hello, who is that? Hello?' The person on the other end was crying and at first, I couldn't make out what they were saying. It was Dinah. 'Aunty Jan, Corey's been shot; he's dead!'

'What?' I wasn't sure what I was hearing. 'Where is he?' She told me where to go, and we got back into the car and drove to Clapton. As we got there, I saw some of his friends sitting on the wall, crying.

The road had been cordoned off with police tape and we couldn't go any further. At that moment, I knew it was true and just wanted to leave. The rest is a blur. I developed an instant headache like never before. I can't remember what happened next, but I went to my mum's house to tell her and then went home.

I sometimes think about the power of words and how important it is to understand the things we say. Corey spoke his destiny; he'd had just a short while of being home before he'd been killed. (The police would have him in a body bag.)

Death and life are in the power of the tongue, and those who love it and indulge it will eat its fruit and bear the consequences of their words.

– Proverbs 18.21

Within no time, the road was filled with people, and the house was packed. I sat on the stairs and watched my whole life in front of me from the beginning. I was dying inside; my worst nightmare had come to life. Just a few weeks before this had happened, I'd had a terrible dream about Corey. I'd dreamt that he was so disfigured and badly hurt it was awful; he told me what happened to him and said, 'Mum, don't let them get away with it.'

I'll never forget how I'd felt in that dream. It had been so real that I'd woken up in shock; my God! But this was not a dream; this was happening; I was already in a terrible state of mind. I'd known things were about to change in my life, but I had not been expecting this. My relationship was at rock bottom and never had I felt so alone, unloved and worthless.

'If he were my son, you would see something!' Over and over, Wade would say that. I did not respond and never said anything out loud, but inside I thought, *He's my son! My son! So, do something then, anything! Even if it's just to feel sorry for me, do something!* Instead, he complained about some of the people coming to the house.

Wade was hardly there; he'd come in late most nights once everyone had gone. He would come in at times and I would be crying. 'What you are crying for now?' he'd ask. My mum was on my side but if she saw me crying, she'd say, 'Janet is the weakest link.' She never meant any harm; she's old school and believes that crying makes you weak. So, I would always try to put on a brave face and hold back my tears, which was hard.

I was grieving the end of the relationship with Wade and mourning the loss of my son at the same time. I didn't have time for any of it; if I did not get myself together, I do not know what would have happened to my children or me.

The day of the funeral came around—it was on the 15th of June. I was in my bedroom getting ready and I could hear the sound of the horse-drawn carriage coming down the road. Standing at the window and looking out, I felt my legs giving way from under me. The rest of my feelings I don't have words to describe.

All I can recall is that I fell to my knees and asked God to hold me up. *Please let me stand today, I can drop down tomorrow, but please God, give me the strength to stand today.* The rest is blank; I have few recollections of that day.

What was going on? What happened to everything working out for good! Where is the good in this? It could not be worse! Why? What did I do to deserve this? I was angry at God, but I needed Him more than ever. If He hadn't shown up for me, I would have died or lost my mind. I wanted to die; I did not see how I could live through this.

I believed that the wages of sin were death, and because I was living in sin, my son had been killed and I was going to be next. After all, that is the word of God, so it must be true; that was my interpretation. I thought it was all my fault. I was ignorant of God's word and did not understand the scriptures. I thought I would die, but God woke me up every morning.

Corey had a brother on his dad's side. His mum and I had become friends when the boys had been young.

One day, she came to visit with her husband and invited me to go to their church. My pastor had been coming to see me at home, but I hadn't gone to church in a while, so I was happy to go with them the coming Sunday. On walking into the church, I felt the presence of God like never before, and I knew that this would be my church home. The more I went to church, the more God ministered to me. I gained strength and an understanding of the scriptures. Corey's death made me see my life differently, and I wanted to reconnect with God on a deeper level.

Because Wade and I lived together, I thought the only way to please God and come out of my sin was to be married. The more I planned in my mind, the more I heard the voice of God speaking to me; telling me, 'This is not your husband, and you are not bound to this relationship.' I heard it almost daily, as things went from bad to worse. I was now in a state of depression and the grief was unbearable but I tried to get on with life the best I could and tried to leave myself with no time to grieve.

One Saturday, I was getting ready to go to a friend's hotel opening. This friend had asked me if I would open the proceedings in prayer. But Wade came home and angrily asked me where I was going. I told him, and he flipped. 'You're not going anywhere!' he shouted at me. My daughter and a friend were downstairs waiting on me while I was upstairs getting into this argument. I thank God she was there because she stopped my son from coming upstairs. He had a knife and was coming to defend me. I was afraid, so to keep the peace, I decided not to go.

That night we argued for hours; the argument turned into a conversation, which eventually led to prayer. It was the first time I had prayed with Wade. Holding his hands, I said, 'God, we cannot carry on like this. We both need peace in this relationship; please let Your will be done.' I prayed something along those lines and decided to give the relationship another try.

The following day, I went to church; it was the 8.30 am service. Just before the end, the Bishop came down off the pulpit and called out to me. 'You,' he said. I turned around to look behind me. 'No, you! Come here.' I left my seat and walked out into the aisle. He began to say, 'God told me to tell you the man you have in your house—there will be no change! He is set in his ways, and there'll be no change!' He said that God said to tell me to run! 'You better run,' he shouted and began to pray in tongues. I could not believe it. Here was the answer to the prayer I'd said last night. But run! What do you mean? Where was I to run? God was trying to get my attention, and I was not listening.

One Sunday evening, I was taking our daughter Chyna to a nativity play at a church in Walthamstow. Don't ask how I ended up in Stoke Newington. Driving down the road, I saw my Wade's car. *Strange. What's he doing down here*? I thought. I called him on the phone, but he didn't answer. I got out of the car and looked in the off-licence across the road; he wasn't in there. I looked around and was about to go back to the car when I heard the Holy Spirit say, 'Walk down a little further.'

'But there's nothing down there!'

'Walk down and cross the road,' I heard clearly, so I kept walking and crossed the road.

Well, lo and behold, there he was in a restaurant having dinner with a man and a woman I knew he'd dated in the past. I'd had no idea they still saw each other, even though rumour had it that they had been together for ages.

Watch and see how the police or ambulance is going to take me out of this restaurant tonight! I thought. I was ready to fight but just as I'd heard God tell me to go there, I heard Him say, 'Turn around and leave. Go back to the car and go where you're going.'

God is so good to me; He had to show me what was going on because I was trying to work things out. Deep down, I did not want another failed relationship, I did not want to give up, but the relationship was clearly over.

'So, you finally left now?' I hear you ask. Well, no, not exactly. I stayed. I hired a private detective to confirm that Wade was, without a doubt, in a relationship with this woman so that I would have good reason to leave.

I used to get dressed when he wasn't around. One day, after taking a shower, I went into the bedroom to get dressed, with a towel wrapped around me. I was about to drop the towel when Wade came into the room. I quickly wrapped it back around myself, and he went mad. 'Why are you hiding from me?' He grabbed the towel and pushed me onto the bed.

God, please don't let this happen to me, please! He was on top of me when I started to pray in my mind as he began to open his trousers. *I was not made with a spirit of fear, but with power, love and a sound mind, this will not happen to me again in my life.* I recited this over and over in my head when suddenly he stopped and went no further. God had stood by His word again.

I got deeper into depression. Everything and anything would start an argument, from shirts not being white to the holes in his socks; it was always my fault. My children were now witnessing what was happening between us in the house. I don't remember what caused this particular fight but one day he hit me with a clothes brush or something that split my head and, with one punch, cracked my rib. With the blood gushing from my head and my daughter screaming, my son came to defend me. 'What have you done to my mum?' It was terrible. Somehow my mum signalled my sister to call the police and the next thing I knew, they were in the room. I am so glad they arrived when they did because this could have been a different story. I have to thank God.

I blamed myself. I had caused the trouble in the relationship; it was me that had changed. Wade was the same man I'd met all those years ago; I was the one moving differently. I didn't know how I would come out of this. There were nights I would leave the bedroom to find my sons sitting facing each other outside my bedroom door, one with a knife, the other with a hammer. When they weren't outside the door, the youngest would sleep with weapons under the pillow.

I have to do something; I can't carry on like this. I had a conversation with my son who said, 'Mum, you are in this because you want to be. You're a strong woman, and you don't ever do anything you don't want to.' That was the turning point for me. I had to think about the effect this was having on my children, not just me, and I made up my mind to leave.

I left the house with nowhere to go and ended up in a bed and breakfast with the kids, then temporary accommodation. *God, I've left my home, and I don't know where I'm going to end up.* However, I really did not care; I just needed peace in my life. I felt like I was losing my mind.

I need to talk about fear for a moment. It's not that I'm giving fear any residence, but I feel I should talk you through how God's word set me free.

For God did not give us a spirit of timidity or cowardice or fear, but [He has given us a spirit] of power and of love and of sound judgment and personal discipline [abilities that result in a calm, well-balanced mind and self-control].

– 2 Timothy 1:7

I rehearsed this scripture over and over in my mind and the more I said it, the more I was faced with situations in which I was afraid and crippled with anxiety. I would ask myself, *What's the worst that can happen? I've been through some terrible things, and I survived.* But my faith was being tested; the enemy would contradict every word God spoke over my life. So, it wasn't enough for me to just read the word of God. It had to become real, and I had to believe it. God was teaching me how to fight, but this time to fight and win!

God said, 'The battle is not yours, Janet; the battle is Mine.' These were deep waters I was in, and it was not just about me. You see, my mother had gone through the same abuse I was going through. This was about generational sin and curses, forefathers' sins, and all that deep stuff that we hope are just myths.

A familiar pattern ran through my bloodline. It was a cycle that needed to be broken, and that I needed to have a fighting spirit to overcome. This was not just for me but my children and my children's children!

After you have suffered for a little while, the God of all grace [who imparts His blessing and favor], who called you to His own eternal glory in Christ, will Himself complete, confirm, strengthen, and establish you [making you what you ought to be].

– 1 Peter 5:10

CHAPTER SEVEN

The House in My Dream

So, there I was, living in one room with my children. If this was not bad enough, the room was on the same road where some of my good friends lived. I was ashamed and would hide from them. I didn't want them to know I was homeless, and I didn't want anybody to see me or the little rusty old car I was now driving. One morning as I was taking Chyna to school, we got in the car and were just about to drive off when we saw one of Corey's friends. I held my head straight, pretending I hadn't seen him. 'Hey, what are you doing around here?' Before I could answer, he noticed the car. 'What are you doing in this old car? Wow! You've gone from riches to rags—ain't it supposed to be rags to riches?'

Then to top it all off, a few days later, I bumped into my friends who lived on the same road. There was no chance to hide but it was a blessing in disguise. God had set me up because He had a plan. The friends were so good to me throughout the time I lived down there, and I could share the gospel with them. Every week they came to church, and Thursday evenings, we would have Bible study and prayer meeting at their house.

As with everything significant in my life, I had a dream. God showed me a house. It was a big double-fronted house with a door in the middle. I entered the house; there was a door on the left and one on the right, and another entry in the middle leading upstairs. I saw a massive landing with rooms and stairs leading to two rooms in the attic. The house was beautiful, but my reality was that they were offering me all these pokey little flats. I was told that they couldn't find anything large enough for us, and I would have to wait. Alternatively, I could separate the family and let my older son get a place of his own. He was only sixteen at the time, so it wasn't an easy decision to make. However, after careful consideration, I decided to do that. Shortly afterwards I got an offer and was excited to go and view the property. I got myself ready, picked up my mum and off we went to the viewing. As we approached the door before even going inside, my mum said, 'This is no good for you,' but I was excited to go in as it was a huge double-fronted house (like in my dream). A woman opened the door, and we went in. There were three flats—one on the left, one on the right. It was a conversion, with the third flat in the middle. As I walked up the stairs, my mum continued, 'No, you can't take this. You're not accustomed to sharing with other people.' Not paying any attention to what she said, I continued up the stairs.

As I turned the corner, I knew this was the house in my dream with the landing and the staircase leading to the other rooms; this was it! OMG! I felt the Holy Spirit confirm to me, 'This is your house!'

'Mum, this is the house!' She wasn't impressed at all.

'This! Janet, you're crazy.'

The house was in a bad state of disrepair and even the woman doing the viewing was surprised at my reaction. 'I have something else I can show you,' she said.

'No! I don't want to see anything else; I like this house.'

She didn't offer it to me; instead, she sent me to view two other properties.

Reluctantly, I went. They were nice, but nothing would change my mind from the first house I had seen. So, I began to pray and claim that house. I was told that they couldn't give it to me because of the disrepair. Somehow, though, the woman called me to meet her and she gave me the keys. I didn't sign any papers or anything, but having the keys meant I could go in there and pray. That was November 2003, and in May 2004, I signed the papers to number 8! My new beginning.

I'll fast forward here and tell you that I still live at number 8 but now, not only do I have the flat upstairs but the flat on the left and the one on the right, too. You see God! The whole house! Yes! The whole house! Just as I saw in my dream. More than ten years later, God came through again, and true to His word, He gave me more than I could ever have imagined. What a blessing. I can see things finally working out for good. However, what I've come to learn along my journey is that with blessings comes warfare and the bigger the warfare, the bigger the blessing. You can also say, the deeper you go in God, the higher He takes you.

I took my time to do up the house. I had no choice; it was in such a bad state, but it was coming along nicely. Chyna was turning thirteen, and for me, this was one of the happiest moments in my life. I can see the hand of God all over her, and He showed me that He is faithful to His word. The curse is broken! For her to get to age thirteen and not have been abused or harmed by anyone is a reason to rejoice and thank God for keeping her as He promised He would. To God be all the glory!

My dreams and visions were coming regularly so I started to keep a dream diary. The majority had scriptures attached, which led me to study my Bible. I had a deep yearning to understand the scriptures and interpret the dreams. Some would be clear as day and come to pass quickly. Others would take long to understand and see the interpretation for. Some don't make any sense, even now.

Back in chapter one, I said that I would tell you how it was that I would come to have such a bond with Miss K's youngest daughter. If you come from a West Indian background, you would probably have heard stories of how they keep dark family secrets hidden—sometimes in a trunk or a suitcase. Well, our household was no different. One day we were playing in the garden, as we often did. I am not sure why we ended up in Miss K's room, but we were in there. We opened the trunk which was full of old photographs, clothes and letters. Amongst them was an album so we took it out, sat down and began to look through it. There were pictures of a baby. 'Who's this?' I asked Miss K's daughter.

'I don't know,' she said.

'This baby looks like you,' I said.

We both agreed the photo was definitely of her.

I asked, 'But where are you, and who are these people holding you?'

We went upstairs to my mum with the album. 'Where unu get dat from?'

'Downstairs in the trunk,' we told her.

'Go and put it back!' she yelled.

'Yeah, but can you tell us who these people are and what she is doing there?'

'Go and put it back!'

As we went to take it back, Mum then sat us down and told us a story. I am unsure of the full story, but by the end, she'd told us we were sisters. 'Sisters!' we cheered together as we held hands skipping in a circle and singing, 'We're sisters, we're sisters!'

'Shhh... It's a secret, and you mustn't tell anyone ever.' We did not ask any more questions; we were both just so happy. We kept that secret between us for years until we were much older.

But how were we sisters? It didn't make sense. How was my dad, her dad? Well, there was a time long ago when we'd all shared a house. I'd been a baby, and my mum had been pregnant with my sister. Turns out my dad had been sleeping with the girl downstairs. She was only 15 or 16 at the time, so it was a big scandal; worse because they were church folks. It was a big embarrassment, so they hid the secret. The pictures we'd seen were of her in a children's home before she'd been adopted. Confused? Well, so was I.

My dad had slept with the young girl who'd lived downstairs, and she got pregnant. All this had been going on while my mum was also pregnant. The babies were born just five months apart, and we'd all shared a house at that time. They'd sent the girl away to have the baby then Miss K had adopted her.

Everyone thought she was Miss K's baby but Miss K was her grandmother.

For years, I thought my dad was a scum bag. He treated my mother terribly and then this sordid secret was also in my mum's face to deal with. You would never have known that all this had taken place. My mum showed that little girl nothing but love and kindness, knowing she was her husband's child.

Years later, we would find out that my dad had known the girl when they'd been in Jamaica. I didn't realise that he'd been nineteen years old at that time; the picture I had all those years was not as bad as I thought. I'm not justifying his behaviour, but I never knew he'd been so young at the time. There was a significant age difference between him and my mum. She'd already had five children in Jamaica, four of whom she'd left with her mother. They had planned to travel to England together, but she became pregnant and had to wait until the baby was born, a little girl, and they left her with his mother.

He had come over a little before her and lived in the house with Miss K, so he'd had plenty of time to carry on. Once my mum had arrived, they'd got married just after I'd been born, but he'd still been sleeping with the girl downstairs. I don't know how they could have kept the secret; their child was the dead stamp of my father; no way could he have denied her.

In chapter two, I also told you about Corey's dad's girlfriend, the one I argued with on the phone. Remember, the one who called me *common chicken girl.* Well, the next time I saw her after that argument was over twenty years later and I bet you couldn't guess where. It was in church! Yes! Church! She now had a son, who is Corey's brother, but had moved on and married a pastor. He was someone I knew from back in the days.

You need to take in this picture. I'm now serving in the church as a peacekeeper, positioned upfront. Seated on the left are her and her husband, and on the right-hand side is the mother of Corey's other brother and her husband; it was them that brought me to Ruach in the first place. We were cool and had a great friendship for many years from when the boys were little.

But this other woman with her facety self was sitting up here all prim and proper like we didn't all three come from the same place and have the one baby father. Right then I felt like I had all those years ago; as she'd said, I was just a *common chicken girl...* 'Where's your husband, Janet?' I thought, *God, I am no different from them, and you have blessed them with good men, husbands, what about me!*

Anyhow, service finished, and we are now walking towards each other. Then her husband, the pastor, said, 'Janet, meet my wife,' or something like that. I cannot tell you precisely what happened; all I know is that in my spirit I felt God say, 'Show nothing but love.'

After all, I am a peacekeeper in a church where 'everybody is somebody'. Almost immediately, I felt different towards her. Those thoughts and feelings I'd had before were gone! Disappeared! Until today we have the most beautiful friendship. You would never believe we were once enemies. God has done great work in us both and I genuinely feel nothing but love from her too. I was also able to meet her son, Corey's brother, for the first time. I was very emotional because he resembles Corey and has some of the same mannerisms. I have so much love for him;

I am just sorry that he and Corey never had the opportunity to know each other well.

Some of the most challenging things for me to deal with happened whilst I was at church. I thought the day I was saved 'for real', everything would change—no more problems. Instead, all hell broke loose; everything that could go wrong did. I felt like my past was constantly being thrown in my face. Stuff I had buried deep would be brought to the surface.

I went to a praise conference; I arrived there excited to hear the singing and the speakers who would be preaching for the evening. I sat close to the front and was enjoying the worship. The Holy Spirit showed up; it was awesome. The host began to greet and acknowledge the delegates and pastors who were there. I heard him say, 'Welcome to this man of God who is doing great things for God in the community; welcome to you and your wife. Stand up and greet the people, my good friend Pastor X.' Well, I almost passed out! I could not believe what I'd heard, but more so, who I was seeing. *Nah, this cannot be so—'Man of God', 'Pastor'! What? You need to add 'Abuser' to that introduction,* I thought. *This 'great man of God' is a rapist!*

How do I know this, you're probably wondering? Well, I knew him from back in the day, as I use to go out with his brother who passed away. I had gone out with some friends and when I'd arrived there, I'd seen him, but he'd looked sad and upset. He'd come and said hello and had asked me if we could talk and to follow him outside. It had been the first time seeing him since his brother had died. I'd gone, not thinking anything of it; by then he'd been close to tears, I'd thought he'd just been upset about his brother and hadn't wanted anyone to see him crying. We'd walked down the road. He hadn't said much; just that he had something for me that his brother hadn't been able to give. We'd stopped walking, and he switched! He pushed me into a dark gap in the road, and he raped me, then went about his business as if nothing happened. I never told a soul of this ordeal, and I never saw him again anywhere, till now.

The feelings I had buried away were back, fresh in my mind. I relived the whole incident over again. I felt like rubbish, useless and good for nothing. I had got what I deserved, that lying voice in my head was telling me, and I was fooling myself to think that God had better for me. Ready to walk out, I heard the Holy Spirit say to me, 'Forgive him.' *Me, forgive him? Surely, he should be asking me for forgiveness, an apology at least.*

'You don't know how he has repented.'

He has never said sorry to me; how can I forgive him? I'm done with all this, and I'm done with the church; I'm not ever going back!

I was troubled for some time; I was hurt and ashamed; even though no one knew what happened, I felt like they did. I was angry at God; why was this happening? 'Forgive him, Janet,' God said. 'Because I have forgiven him and changed his life.

Old things have passed away and have been made new in Christ Jesus.' I can tell you that this was not what I wanted to hear.

I don't know when or how it happened, but the next time I saw him, we spoke. He invited me to something he was doing relating to gun crime in the area. He was a changed man actively serving God and the community. Those feelings that brought me down were gone. I forgave him—no anger, no bitterness, free! Free to get on with my life. I was leaving the past behind, stepping into the future through the power of the Holy Spirit and forgiveness.

Therefore, if anyone is in Christ that is, grafted in, joined to Him by faith in Him as Saviour, he is a new creature [reborn and renewed by the Holy Spirit]; the old things [the previous moral and spiritual condition] have passed away. Behold, new things have come [because spiritual awakening brings a new life].

– 2 Corinthians 5:17

CHAPTER EIGHT

'Give Janet a Plane'

I was serving in the church and on leadership training at Brixton Bible Institute. Outside of church, I was training with the Citizens Advice Bureau to be a Generalist Advisor. It was then that God placed a vision in my heart to do something in the community. Many mothers are going through the same things and losing children through gang culture and postcode wars. Gun and knife crime is prevalent among our young people, and they're filling up the prisons. Young girls are being abused both sexually and physically; teenage pregnancy is at a record high. That was the beginning of 'Mothers with a Voice'. My life was back on course; at last. I started sharing my story on different platforms.

I was invited to attend the Ask, Seek, Knock Tour in 2006 hosted by David Lammy with Jesse Jackson. Church leaders and politicians from all around the country were in attendance. I could not believe it when the invitation came. To say I was nervous was an understatement! Me, you know, going to sit around the table with all these dignitaries in Westminster! Wow, only God! I fixed myself up, put on my suit and some little high heels, slicked back my hair and headed to Westminster. When I entered the room, my heart was beating so fast. *Pull yourself together, girl, you got this.* I stood there looking around in awe. There were a few people I recognised from within the community. I could tell by the way they looked at me that they were thinking, *What is she doing here*? Worse, because I had a seat at the table, and they were standing. A lady took my name and led me to my seat.

Janet Wright, Mothers with a Voice, was written on the place card. It was a huge table; people began to take their seats. Once we were all seated, it was time to introduce ourselves. Everyone had a title: Bishop, Pastor and MP. *What do I say when it's my turn?* I was so nervous I could have run out of the room. With my mouth as dry as chips and in my telephone voice, I introduced myself: 'Janet Wright, founder of Mothers with a Voice'. *That wasn't so bad*, I said to myself as I reached for a glass of water.

My life finally had some purpose and I was in a good place when I got a phone call. My son had been stabbed. My God! *Please!* I cried as I prayed. *God, you promised me that I would not go through these things again; my son would not die like this!*

I made my way to the hospital, where I was met by one of the pastors from church and he prayed for him. The attackers had cut the arteries in his wrists and cut his face quite badly. He needed to have surgery to repair the damage, so he was moved to the London Hospital. No sooner had he recovered from his injuries when the next thing I knew, he was in prison. Again, it brought me back to Corey being in prison. *Where are you, God?* I was reliving it all. Every pain I felt, every emotion, was like an unbearable weight on my shoulders. I did not finish my training with the Citizens Advice Bureau as I went to the prison almost every day whilst he was on remand. I continued to serve in the church but I moved from hospitality to the spiritual mediation department, first as an intercessor, then later as a prayer counsellor.

During that season, amid all the turmoil, I had more and more dreams and visions, and almost all of them would come to pass. Brixton Bible Institute had a course that was about to start, so I decided to enrol in the school of prophets.

One day I was at church, the service was coming to an end, and the preacher made the altar call. I took my place in the front, waiting for anyone who would come for prayer. I was standing directly in front of Pastor Enid and as the people began to make their way to the altar, she started walking towards me. Pastor Enid is someone God has used to counsel me throughout my spiritual journey. She put her arms around me and started praying. I don't remember much of what was said, apart from *Lord strengthen her.* With her hand on my stomach, she continued to pray hard! *Lord strengthen her.* It was as if she imparted something inside me.

I believe that God showed her something in the Spirit because I was about to go through another devastating season in my life, and God knew that I would need strength to get through it.

Shortly after that Sunday, my mum had a stroke. It was her second one and had a much larger impact on her health, so I moved into her house to care for her. From the stroke, she developed vascular dementia. Her condition quickly deteriorated and she was soon unable to speak or do anything for herself. To see her completely helpless and change in that way was tough for me.

For almost three years, I could not go to church. I didn't even get the chance to apply for the school of prophets, and it didn't stop there. In June 2011, my son was shot whilst at home, and later that year, my mum passed away peacefully in my arms. What was I going to do without my mum? She'd been my best friend and my support in every way. She'd encouraged me, and she'd believed I could do anything.

I remember one of her sayings: 'Give Janet the plane, and she can fly it.' She'd never accepted the words *I can't* from me because she'd always believed I could achieve anything I set my mind to.

Every time I got my life on track, all hell would break loose around me and I lurched from one tragedy to the next. You see, the enemy has nothing new and comes at you with the same old things. He tries to keep you in that place in your mind to retain every bad or negative thing that has ever happened to you. It is so that you never fulfil your God-given purpose and the plans He has for your life.

Throughout the years and at times when I felt isolated, alone, and sometimes embarrassed or ashamed to talk to anyone, I would have conversations with God. I did not see it as prayer—I was just talking.

What I have come to realise is that prayer is a form of communication; talking to God and God talking back to you.

Many people, as I did, feel like they cannot pray or need a priest or pastor to pray for them. Some believe that if they don't go to a church, God does not listen to them. Or they are intimidated because they do not sound like the people they hear in church. But Christ is our High Priest, and we can all come boldly before the throne of grace. Praying is something we are all called to do. So, here I was again, hearing God saying to continue with the vision He had given me and share everything I had been taught. I felt that this was my last chance to do as I was told, so, in 2017, I started prayer ministry school, at Ellel Ministries. It would be the last time that they would run that course and I had the last space. I enrolled to attend with no idea where the money would come from to pay the fees, much less how I would get there, but God had already made a way for me. All I had to do was take the first steps and go. There was a payment I could not make, and I called to tell them I would not make it because I did not have the money. The lady on the phone asked for my details and said, 'This has already been paid in full.' Someone had anonymously made the payment. I have no idea who did it. All I know is that throughout my attendance at Ellel, God would show up for me so I could complete the course. Not only did I finish training, but I also received deliverance from the effects of all the trauma in my past. God healed me from the grief and heartache I was still carrying.

In April 2018, I went to church. The woman of God preached such a powerful word that confirmed everything God had been saying to me. She made an altar call. I took myself up there so fast, I was the first person there! I was not expecting anything; I was just so grateful, and I wanted to lay everything down at the altar and leave it there. But God spoke to me through the pastor. She told me that this time next year, I wouldn't feel the same, that God was going to heal my broken heart, and things were about to change.

You see, I was just living, waking up every day, getting on with life, but with no hope, no dreams and no expectations. I believed that I had my lot in life and would say, 'God has done enough for me, so if He does nothing else that is fine.' This was it for me, and I was quite happy to carry on this way. However, all that did change.

At the same time the following year, April 2019, it was eighteen years since Corey had been killed. I had decided prior to the day that I would go to the cemetery. It's not a place I visit often, in fact hardly at all, but this year I felt the need to go, and I'm so glad I went.

Instead of feeling that sad, heavy weight of grief, I felt God's love surround me. I am alive and of sound mind, and He has kept me. I have gone full circle and have been given another chance to a fresh start. Everything the enemy has stolen; God has given back to me.

I am a new person on the inside, full of life and looking forward to what God has in store for me. The pain I felt in my heart has gone and my dreams and hopes have been restored. Because God loves me unconditionally, I can now love myself and believe I am worthy, and I have a purpose.

Epilogue

Writing this book has been difficult for me. The years have passed and to revisit my painful past was uncomfortable but completely necessary for me to do.

I was born into a dysfunctional family and raised by a single parent. Sexually abused and excluded from school, I then became a teenage single mother. I've been physically abused, incarcerated and homeless, and lost my firstborn to gun crime. I then cared for my mother until she died in my arms. I am now the full-time carer for my younger sister, Veronica, who has special needs and complex medical issues.

Despite how my life began and the trauma and abuse I'd been through, God filled me with His amazing grace. He chose me to fulfil His purpose on this earth. He forgave all my sins. He turned my life around and loved me when I believed I was unlovable. He saved and set me free!

God has taught me so much through His unfailing love; I now have forgiveness in my heart, which has been one of the keys to many breakthroughs for me. My boys' father is not the man he was back then, and I am sure he has a story to tell.

We now have a great relationship and this was not written with any malicious intent towards anyone mentioned other than it being part of my story. I take full responsibility for the choices I made and accept that I never gave the fathers of my children any choice. It was selfish of me to place the responsibility on them when I made all the decisions by myself.

We all have been wronged at some point in our lives. Most of you, probably, have been seriously hurt by someone who has never apologised or attempted to do anything to make it right. One of the hindrances to letting that hurt and bitterness go is the justified conviction that justice should be done. People can't just get away with the horrible things they do, we think. That is what stands in the way of forgiveness. We hold on to the anger and replay the story over and over, continuing to carry those feelings of hurt when they were wrong! *How can they be so happy now when I am so miserable?* It's not about who is wrong or right. We have to give it to God, lay it all down; it does not mean they have not done you wrong, or that they will get away with it. No, it simply means when you lay it down, God will pick up; it is you taking a deep breath, maybe for the first time in years and feeling like now, at last, you can be free.

For if you forgive others their trespasses
[their reckless and willful sins],
your heavenly Father will also forgive you.

But if you do not forgive others
[nurturing your hurt and anger with the result
that it interferes with your relationship with God],
then your Father will not forgive your trespasses.

– Matthew 6:14-15

Not only did it take me a long time to write this book because of the pain of my past, I also struggled to finish it because I kept telling myself there was more to add, that the story was not over. I had been waiting for the fairy tale ending where I could tell you that I'd met someone, and we were now happily married. Well, that is not how it ends, because this is not a fairy tale, so I had to address issues I still had about being single.

I have been waiting for God to bless me with a husband, that is the only thing missing in my life. But if I'm honest, I was not waiting; I was praying but looking for myself. I did meet someone a few years back that I honestly believed was 'the one'. I found myself reverting to my old ways, getting comfortable, ready to give my all with nothing in return. But God says, 'He who finds a wife, finds a good thing', not 'SHE who finds', so that season for me was full of heartache, frustration and disappointments. God had to bring me to a place where I understand that being single does not defy who I am and certainly, does not mean I am not blessed. There is nothing wrong with me and in the fullness of His time, my prayers will be answered, and the right person will come into my life.

I know many of you have a story that is similar to, if not the same as, mine. You feel alone and unloved, broken-hearted and believe there is no hope for you.

I want you to remember that…

1. *God is with you every step of the way.* He knows where you are, and everything you're facing; and He is providing for and protecting you along the way.

2. *He has a purpose for every trial and all the challenges you face.* In order to make you His useful and effective representative, God trains you in the fires of adversity. This is because there is nothing that deepens your understanding, stirs your compassion for others, and shows you what's truly important than the way pain does.

3. *You're in a spiritual battle (Eph. 6:12).* You have a real enemy who strikes at the core of who you are. How does he do so? Through what you think and believe (2 Cor. 10:4-5). There's no more effective time for the devil to

discourage and torment you than when you're waiting on God. He knows exactly how to pinpoint the most painful, vulnerable places in your life and lead you to despair. But through Jesus' example in Matthew 4, you can resist the devil's disheartening lies with courage and the powerful truth of Scripture.

4. *You must express thanks to God, regardless of what happens (1 Thess. 5:18).* You must give thanks in every situation and delay you face, and trust in God who will ultimately bring you through.

Take courage—there's a limit to the delays and sufferings in your life. They will only continue as long as is necessary for God to accomplish His purposes in you (Psalm 138:8). If you'll remain courageous and faithful, trusting God to guide you through the difficult times of your life, then He'll do great and wonderful things, in and through you.

And He'll move you from despair to the wonderful place where all of His promises for you are fulfilled.

I hope that by reading my story you can see how God has been the source of strength in my life and ever-present help in my times of need. He never left me, and He will never leave you.

Make a decision today to make Christ Lord of your life. He is waiting for you with open arms.

Inspiring Verses About Grace

From the NIV

Acts 20:24

However, I consider my life worth nothing to me; my only aim is to finish the race and complete the task the Lord Jesus has given me—the task of testifying to the good news of God's grace.

Hebrews 4:16

Let us then approach God's throne of grace with confidence, so that we may receive mercy and find grace to help us in our time of need.

Numbers 6:24-26

The Lord bless you and keep you; the Lord make his face shine on you and be gracious to you; the Lord turn his face toward you and give you peace.

Ephesians 2:4-5

But because of his great love for us, God, who is rich in mercy, made us alive with Christ even when we were dead in transgressions—it is by grace you have been saved.

Psalm 103:8

The Lord is compassionate and gracious, slow to anger, abounding in love.

1 Peter 5:10

And the God of all grace, who called you to his eternal glory in Christ, after you have suffered a little while, will himself restore you and make you strong, firm and steadfast.

Titus 2:11-12

For the grace of God has appeared that offers salvation to all people. It teaches us to say "No" to ungodliness and worldly passions, and to live self-controlled, upright and godly lives in this present age.

Matthew 6:14

For if you forgive other people when they sin against you, your heavenly Father will also forgive you.

2 Timothy 1:9

He has saved us and called us to a holy life—not because of anything we have done but because of his own purpose and grace. This grace was given us in Christ Jesus before the beginning of time.

Isaiah 30:18

Yet the Lord longs to be gracious to you; therefore, he will rise up to show you compassion. For the Lord is a God of justice. Blessed are all who wait for him!

Romans 6:14

For sin shall no longer be your master, because you are not under the law, but under grace.

Revelation 22:21

The grace of the Lord Jesus be with God's people. Amen.

Romans 3:23-24

For all have sinned and fall short of the glory of God, and all are justified freely by his grace through the redemption that came by Christ Jesus.

Romans 6:15

What then? Shall we sin because we are not under the law but under grace? By no means!

Ephesians 2:8-9

For it is by grace you have been saved, through faith—and this is not from yourselves, it is the gift of God—not by works, so that no one can boast.

2 Chronicles 30:9

For the Lord your God is gracious and compassionate. He will not turn his face from you if you return to him.

John 3:16

For God so loved the world that he gave his one and only Son, that whoever believes in him shall not perish but have eternal life.

Philemon 1:25

The grace of the Lord Jesus Christ be with your spirit.

1 Peter 1:13

Therefore, with minds that are alert and fully sober, set your hope on the grace to be brought to you when Jesus Christ is revealed at his coming.

Romans 5:15

But the gift is not like the trespass. For if the many died by the trespass of the one man, how much more did God's grace and the gift that came by the grace of the one man, Jesus Christ, overflow to the many!

Proverbs 28:13

Whoever conceals their sins does not prosper, but the one who confesses and renounces them finds mercy.

Romans 5:21

So that, just as sin reigned in death, so also grace might reign through righteousness to bring eternal life through Jesus Christ our Lord.

2 Corinthians 12:9

But he said to me, "My grace is sufficient for you, for my power is made perfect in weakness." Therefore, I will boast all the more gladly about my weaknesses, so that Christ's power may rest on me.

2 Peter 3:18

But grow in the grace and knowledge of our Lord and Saviour Jesus Christ. To him be glory both now and forever! Amen.

Philippians 4:23

The grace of the Lord Jesus Christ be with your spirit.
Amen.

Romans 16:20

The God of peace will soon crush Satan under your feet. The grace of our Lord Jesus be with you.

Galatians 2:21

I do not set aside the grace of God, for if righteousness could be gained through the law, Christ died for nothing!

Write the vision down

Then the LORD ANSWERED ME AND SAID,

'Write the vision

And engrave it plainly on [clay] tablets

So that the one who reads it will run'.

– Habakkuk 2:2

Notes

Notes

Notes

Notes

Notes

Prayer List

References

The Bible Panorama, Gerard Chrispin (DayOne Publications, 2015)

Devotional: Waiting on God, Charles F Stanley (Thomas Nelson, 2020)

Lightning Source UK Ltd.
Milton Keynes UK
UKHW021111180821
389055UK00012B/818